MW01514608

NAKED FEET LIVING

FINDING YOUR REAL SELF
AT WORK AND IN LIFE

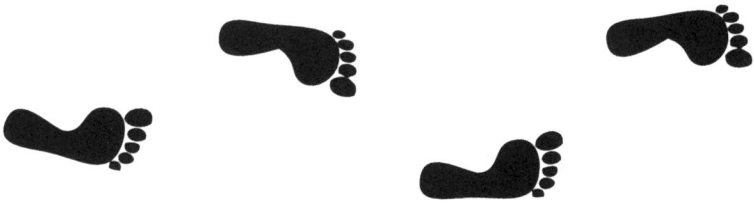

LISA SHASKY AND
CYNDI STREID

Copyright © 2011 Naked Feet Living, Inc.

Copyright © 2011 Naked Feet Living, Inc.
All rights reserved.

ISBN: 1460963830
ISBN-13: 9781460963838

WHAT OTHER READERS ARE SAYING ABOUT *Naked Feet Living*

"Lisa Shasky and Cyndi Streid have written a fabulous book that invites the reader to enjoy who they are at their core. Naked Feet Living is an excellent guide to assist those who want to replace their judgmental thoughts with new playful, empowering stories. This book takes the reader on a journey of self-discovery through practical processes and fun shift moves as you break down and reframe the stories that have defined you. A must read if you are ready to laugh at your own stories and use them for your personal growth and professional transformation."

Anna McGrath
Founder, President
WonderWorks Consulting

"In these fast paced times of never ending emails, conference culls, meetings, and business travel Naked Feet Living is a must read and an important reminder that life is too short to not have fun at work. The authors utilize real life examples in interesting stories to illustrate behaviors that we have all exhibited at one time or another in the workplace but probably didn't recognize. I found it to be an easy and thought provoking read whether you are an employee, a mentor, a mentee, an executive or all of the above."

Denise Ruggiero
VP - Research, Policy & Regulatory Counsel
Farmers Group Inc.

"It's rare to find a book that combines captivating stories, practical business wisdom, and immediately applicable strategies for improving your life on and off the job. But that is exactly what Naked Feet Living has accomplished. With so many good books on the market and so little time to read them all, you need to focus on the 'best' books. I would put this book in the 'best' category. You'll be better off for reading it. I know I am."

Dr. Alan R. Zimmerman
Certified Speaking Professional
Speaker Hall of Fame

"Not only is Naked Feet Living engaging to read, the stories and writing evokes vivid visuals of the narrative that takes the reader to the moment. The questions, the suggestions for "getting naked" really takes the reader to that place of thinking of what it means to let yourself go and be who you are by "getting naked". Metaphorically while naked feet is about finding your real you, it's as much about allowing yourself to be exposed and "naked" to others so they too can see the real you."

Linda Akutagawa
Sr. Vice President
Leadership Education for Asian Pacifics, Inc. (LEAP)

"Naked Feet Living creates a journey of self improvement based on who we are and how we would like to be. Life should be about getting to be a better person at home and at work. This book is a must read if you're serious about being a better person."

Jerry L. Cooper, Ph.D.
University of Missouri-Kansas City

ACKNOWLEDGEMENTS

We are indebted to so many who helped this book move from a crazy idea among friends to a reality. Writing a book is not a one (or two) person task, it truly takes a team to pull this all together. To our family, friends, colleagues, coaches and mentors we thank you with all our hearts for listening to us, encouraging us to continue and expressing your belief in this book in so many ways big and small. To those of you whose stories are included here, either directly or indirectly, thank you for your example and for being authentically you. Our thanks also to our editor, Kathy Carter, who was able to make sense of our writing styles and somehow merge them into one. And last, but definitely not least, we owe a huge debt of gratitude to Jane Flanders Osborn, the creative genius behind the cover design.

CONTENTS

Acknowledgements V

Introduction 1

1. Getting in the Mood at Work and in Life 3

2. The Land of Make-Believe Between Your Ears 7

3. Sod Farm – The Art of Effective Storytelling 13

4. Don't Let the Bully Steal Your Gumdrops 17

5. Everyone Has Their Own Crap 23

6. Island Living 29

7. The Connection Game.. 35

8. Creating Memories... 39

9. Setting Boundaries with Others 45

10. You Deserve a Life You Love 51

11. Choosing Your Life 57

12. Finding Your Voice 65

13. Sharing the Journey 71

14. Curveballs and Sucker Punches 77

Epilogue: Final Thoughts on Getting Real 85

INTRODUCTION

Naked feet. What does this image make you think of? Perhaps it conjures up childhood memories of green blades of grass tickling the soles of your feet as you walked or ran across a lawn. Or perhaps it's the soothing sensation of sand as it molds to the shape of your foot . . . sand squeezing between your toes . . . seeing your bare footprint in the wet sand. Naked feet. It may call to mind standing barefoot on a boat, feeling the speed and sense of freedom underneath you . . . the fun of a pedicure . . . the occasional game of "footsie" with someone special. There's something about naked feet that makes you want to smile, relax, and laugh.

Now contrast this with tight shoes, cramped toes, high heels, and jobs that require you to be on your toes all day, literally and figuratively. Do you feel the difference in your thoughts, feelings, facial expression, and sense of fun?

Which of these two mindsets—naked feet or tight shoes— sounds more like how you are at work? If you're like many of us, you're probably more "tight shoes" when you're in work mode. We've been taught to be professional, to act seriously to be taken seriously, and that the stakes are high, so hard work, a furrowed brow, and a nose to the grindstone are required.

The problem is that you may end up with a split personality. There is your work personality—all serious, tight shoes and cramped toes—and your "real life" personality that wants to run through the grass, feel the sand massage your feet, and laugh out loud.

Now if you're really honest with yourself, wouldn't you be happier if you could bring more of your "naked feet" side into your work life? Wouldn't the people you work with be happier and more productive being around you?

The purpose of this book is to help you bring more of your naked feet side into your life—especially at work. Our hope is that you'll read this with a good friend, a mentor, a close coworker, or someone else that you trust and feel comfortable with. We recommend that you read and discuss one chapter per session.

The questions at the end of each chapter are meant to be talked about and explored with each other, leading you down a path of self-discovery and new ideas. You don't have to answer every question—pick the ones that apply to where you are in your life right now or that most challenge you. Feel free to probe each other, ask your own follow-up questions, and encourage each other to go deeper. You'll both learn more in the process.

Remember that just like wandering down a sandy beach or sauntering through the grass in your bare feet, reading this book is a journey. Take time to enjoy the process, and the end will take care of itself.

Here's to naked feet and having more fun at work...and in life!

CHAPTER 1

GETTING IN THE MOOD AT WORK AND IN LIFE

No doubt you've picked up this book eager to find lots of practical tips and ideas. You are sitting at your desk or at a conference table at the office, or maybe you're at a local coffee shop—eager to get started learning.

Well, as in other areas of life (including romance), diving right in isn't always the best route to take. A little mental fore-play can make the whole journey that much more enjoy-able. So let's take a little time to get in the mood—envisioning what you are hoping to achieve and engaging some of your senses in the experience.

Start by picturing a perfect day. Here's mine: It's early in the morning and no one else is up yet. I'm sitting on the edge of the dock with my feet dangling in the water. The sun is shining down from just above the trees, not too hot and not too cool. I feel a slight breeze and hear the wa-ter gently lapping against the shore. My bare feet aimlessly swirl the water and kick slowly back and forth. I feel totally relaxed and happy, free to let my mind wander. Problems seem smaller, solutions more obvious, and the future more certain. Every so often I like to lift my feet and watch as the water runs off, trickles between my toes, and makes patterns in the water below. Occasionally a fish jumps in the water or a duck floats aimlessly by. Birds sing in the trees, and I feel an amazing calm.

Now, describe *your* perfect day—the type of day when you feel the most relaxed and the most like your real self. Really paint the picture or describe the movie you see in your mind. What does it look like? What sounds do you hear? Do you smell anything? Who else is with you? What are they doing? What are you doing? What are you feeling and thinking? Maybe it's playing with your kids and hearing their squeals of laughter, or enjoying a round of golf with friends on a perfect summer morning. Perhaps it's sitting on the patio at your favorite restaurant, watching a beautiful sunset with reds, purples, oranges, and yellows splattered across the evening sky. Whatever it is for you, I'll bet that even as you think about it now, your breathing has slowed, the tension has left your face muscles, and you feel happier and more relaxed.

We've asked many people to describe their perfect day, and it's amazing how often their description includes something about their feet. Most often they describe being barefoot—whether walking on the beach, feeling the grass on their soles, taking their shoes off at the end of the day, taking a walk in flip-flops in their favorite park, and so on.

Even if your perfect day doesn't include bare—or naked—feet, can you relate the day you imagined to this naked feet state of being? You are totally relaxed and unselfconscious. This is when the real you comes out. If people at work see you as serious, this is when you let your hair down. If people normally see you as self-controlled and up-tight, this is when you might karaoke with the kids or laugh hysterically at the latest sitcom. Perhaps others see you as outgoing and able to easily share your opinions. In the naked feet state of being, you may be quieter and more thoughtful.

It takes a lot of energy to keep up these two (or more) sides of yourself. Having a clear and specific picture of what you want for yourself—whether at work, outside of work, or both—will motivate you to make it a reality. Knowing who you are today and who you want to be will energize you for the journey ahead. When you know the destination is a great place, you can't wait to get there!

GETTING NAKED

1. Describe your perfect day of fun. What does it look like? Feel like? Who is with you? What are you doing? What are you wearing? What are you thinking about? What is it about this day that makes you so happy?

2. Make two lists on a sheet of paper, labeling the left side "My Naked Feet State of Being" and the right side "My Work Self." What words would you use to describe each

of these? Is one list more appealing to you than the other? How would you benefit from incorporating more of a naked feet mindset into your life at work and outside of work? How would those around you benefit? Would your business benefit? How?

3. Describe your perfect day at work—or if you prefer, imagine the job you want to have a year from now. What does your workplace look like? Who is with you? What are you doing? How do you feel? Now ask yourself what you are doing to make that picture a reality.

4. A variation from a combined personal/work perspective: What would you have in your perfect life? Who would be with you? What would you be focused on in your work? How would you spend your recreational time? Where would you live? How would you live? Who would you be? Who could you become?

CHAPTER 2

THE LAND OF MAKE-BELIEVE BETWEEN YOUR EARS

I'm afraid of heights. My mom is afraid of heights also, so I figure it's some kind of genetic thing. Once while attending a conference in a large hotel in Chicago, I approached my room on the twenty-first floor and noticed the floor-to-ceiling window at the end of the hall. The view was spectacular, I'm sure, but all I saw was that the floor suddenly seemed to tilt at a forty-five-degree angle toward the window. I had the overwhelming sensation that I was sliding down the hall, about to crash through the window and plunge to my death. It took quite a bit of coaxing by those I was traveling with to get me safely down the hall and into my room.

I also don't like to climb ladders beyond the third or fourth rung. And I love to go hiking in beautiful places like the red rock area in Sedona, Arizona, or the mountains of Colorado, but I've been known to totally freeze in my tracks when the hike requires navigating a narrow path with a sharp drop-off on one side or a suspended bridge over a deep chasm. So see? I'm afraid of heights.

So what's your story? Maybe you're not athletic or not a people person. Maybe you're good with numbers or creative. Perhaps you are too tall or short, too heavy, not heavy enough, too serious, a comedian, or the smart one.

The funny thing is that not only do we have a certain way of seeing ourselves, but we also have elaborate stories that support this view. Take my stories of close encounters with heights—I can recall vividly the many times I've been stopped in my tracks, frozen in place by this fear. I'll bet you too have elaborate stories to support your view of yourself.

The thing about many of these stories is they have life only because we choose to give them life. We continue to tell ourselves the stories that support our conclusion that we're afraid of heights, creative, too serious, good with people, or whatever it may be, and thus those ideas become real to us. Our stories are a mix of positive traits and negative ones. Unfortunately, we're probably most skilled at the stories that support our negative traits. These stories become like fairy tales—full of vivid images, interesting characters, and just enough reality mixed in to pull us into the land of make-believe. But unlike fairy tales, as these stories are told and retold to ourselves and others, they take on a life of their own. We begin to live as if they are reality.

A theory I had about my work for a long time was that "the reward for good work is more work to do." Now this may sound all right on the surface, but it was really a cynical theory that meant the *punishment* for good work is more and more work to do. I started to attach stories to this theory: the time I had worked very hard to turn around the morale of my team, only to be given more people to manage and new sets of problems to overcome; spending countless hours researching and drafting a major recommendation for a staffing restructure, only to be assigned to lead a study reexamining our area's entire strategic direction—and all of this on top of day-to-day management of my operation and resolving customer service problems. I could go on and on naming times I felt work had been "piled on" simply because I'd done good work previously.

Now what if I replace this reward/punishment story with a more empowering story? How about "I am good at what I do, and those I work with recognize my talents. New assignments come my way so that I can teach and influence others." This story puts me in the driver's seat and makes me feel more energized.

Our stories about ourselves and others are very powerful. They influence how we act, what we believe, whom we spend time with, and what we choose to do or not do. They can put unnecessary limits on what we can become and our overall experience of life. Don't fall into the trap of thinking all the thoughts that spin around in your head are reality. We all tell ourselves stories, so why not choose stories that empower you?

Back to my story about being afraid of heights. Recently I took a rock-climbing lesson, and I didn't die! I actually climbed quite high up the rock wall. The whole time I was thinking, "This is a fun challenge of my physical skills, and I'll know how well I did by how high I'm able to climb." I was so busy learning the rope techniques for climbing and holding another climber that I never had time to tell myself my old "fear of heights" story. I was engrossed in the challenge, enjoying my time with good friends and the excitement of trying something new.

The power of the stories we tell ourselves is amazing. Do you choose to continue the old, limiting stories or to discover the power of new stories?

GETTING NAKED

1. What are the negative stories you're telling yourself— work-related or non-work-related? List some of your long-held stories. Next to each one, write a new story—something that empowers you to break out of old boundaries and see yourself or a situation in a new way. For example:

CURRENT STORY	NEW STORY
I am afraid of heights— remember the hotel, Colorado, crossing that old bridge.	I can climb a rock wall, and I had fun challenging myself to climb higher than I did last time.
The punishment for good work is more work to do.	I am recognized for my talents and given the opportunity to help others learn.

Work is serious, and I need to act seriously in order to be respected.	I can smile and have fun at work and still get results. I enjoy celebrating small victories and large ones with my coworkers—such as a high five, a cheer, or going out to lunch (and not talking shop!). I'll actually be more respected for being "real."

2. Who are you as a person? Write down the first five words that come to mind. Don't over think this or write down what you "should" think about yourself—just list the first five words that come up for you. Now stop writing—no changes. What do these words say about you? Are you surprised by anything that is—or is not—on the list?

3. To take this another step, ask a few others to write down five words that describe you. Try to choose people from different aspects of your life—perhaps a coworker, an employee, or your boss; your spouse, partner, boy-friend, or girlfriend; and a parent or sibling. The same rule applies—ask them to write down the first five words that come to them to describe you. Assure them there are no wrong or right answers.

4. If you have done number 2 and number 3, compare the lists. Is anything surprising? Choose your "top five"—the five words from all the responses (including your own) that best describe how you want to be. What stories

do you tell yourself that are keeping you from becoming the person that those words describe? What new stories could you replace them with that are more empowering?

CHAPTER 3

SOD FARM—THE ART OF EFFECTIVE STORYTELLING

Have you ever had a friend who seems to understand you right away? Very early in your relationship, this person starts to finish your sentences just the way you would. He or she knows what type of mood you're in just by looking at you or hearing your voice, and knows just the thing that will settle your soul back into its natural rhythm. I'm not talking about your life partner, but rather a pal or a coworker, someone you spend time with outside of your primary relationship . . . someone who just "gets" you.

I think these people are there for all of us. The gift is to recognize them and hang on to these relationships through the ups and downs of life.

I have been blessed to have not one, but two such people in my life to date. I count myself lucky; but at the same time, I am conscious of the need to stay awake in each relationship so that we both continue to grow and prosper from our time together. Being known so well by someone can lead to complacency and to "communication laziness." This realization came to me during an ordinary car ride with "my person."

Our journey was not unlike others we had taken. We were headed to a neighboring city some sixty miles away to run an errand. We spent the drive catching up on all things personal and professional, getting into our comfortable groove of conversation.

As we drew closer to our destination, we started to take the back roads into the city—a route I was very familiar with, since I used to travel this way daily to my workplace. On one such country road is a sod farm. It's really no more than a parcel of land covered in grass, with a gravel drive, a loading area, and a small shack that I presume serves as its office.

As we passed the farm, I sharply executed a well-choreographed swing of my arm above and across the steering wheel, perfectly timed with the pronouncement of "That is a sod farm." By this simple declaration, I expected my person—the person who had verbalized many of my thoughts before I had the courage to do so—to gain the full experience of that sod farm as I had seen it change over the eighteen months I had traversed these back roads to work. I was sure she "saw" everything I had seen: The tractor turning the soil on the morning drive to work and the fully seeded strips of ground on the return trip home that night. My wonderment at the tractor plowing the field on wet, soggy days and my calculation of yield lost to extended periods of time underwater when the spring rains would not let up. The sight of the eighteen-wheeler with a flatbed trailer awaiting its load on the gravel drive while the sod ripper churned up rolls of grass from the field. The rich black soil just stripped of its deep green top, in contrast to vast areas of lush grass awaiting their date with destiny. My contemplation of how this field of grass remained such a vibrant, healthy green through hot summer months when no irrigation system was readily noticeable. The quick turnaround time for preparing and reseeding the soil throughout the spring, summer, and fall months so that a harvest could be executed every six to eight weeks.

All of this flashed through my mind as I made my five-word declaration of "That is a sod farm." However, as I looked at my person so I could witness her new enlightenment regarding this topic, I was met with a blank stare. By the noticeable silence and the sight of her mouth hanging half open as she started to articulate "Huh?" it became quickly apparent—I had left her waiting for the rest of the story.

After enjoying a good laugh about my inability to tell a complete story and the utterly dumbfounded look on her face, we started a new conversation about sod farms and my experience of them. It is safe to say that my person left this conversation with a whole new understanding of sod farms (whether she wanted it or not!), and I learned a valuable lesson regarding communication.

I learned that no matter how well you know someone or think that person knows you, effective storytelling takes time—time to "paint your picture," touching the senses and awakening the feelings of your audience. Checking for understanding along the way allows you and your audience to stay on the same wavelength so they experience your story as intended. Your audience, however, will have their own experience of your story through your sharing. They will know not only your story topic, but <u>you</u> on a new level.

GETTING NAKED

1. Do you have a person who just "gets" you? If so, do you take the time to nurture this relationship? If so, how? If not, why not?

2. If you don't currently have a person who "gets" you, have you in the past? If so, what changed? Is the relationship worth rekindling?

3. When has your storytelling led to new understanding for your audience? What did you include in your story? What personal thoughts and feelings did you include?

4. When has your storytelling fallen flat? What was different about this attempt at telling your story?

5. Have you shared a story and not been understood by your audience as you intended? If so, what assumptions did you make about yourself or your audience as a result of that experience? What have you done differently going forward?

CHAPTER 4

DON'T LET THE BULLY
STEAL YOUR GUMDROPS

I t all started innocently enough. It was the day before Thanksgiving break, and the school was teetering on the edge of chaos, every student and teacher anxiously awaiting the sound of the day's final bell. I was an excited second grader about to take my latest art project home for the holiday: a construction-paper Thanksgiving turkey, complete with gumdrop feet that would allow my creation to proudly stand in the middle of our dining room table for the family feast.

As we were let out of the building, my friend and I decided to take the long way home, expanding my half-mile walk by another quarter mile. I was so happy with my latest piece of art. I replayed in my mind how I had strategically picked my turkey's feet out of the myriad of gumdrops that had been scattered about our workspace a couple of days earlier. Fred (all turkeys need a name!) had one cherry and one grape foot, because everyone knows those two flavors are the best, so I scored big-time when I wrangled these gumdrops for my own. There would be no orange, lemon, or lime gumdrops for Fred. With cherry and grape feet, Fred was assured to be the hit of the party and my finest work yet.

About halfway home, my friend and I picked up a "tail"—a boy who typified every young student's worst nightmare of the school bully. You know the type: twice as big as us in every sense. When he started to call out in a taunting way, I knew we should have taken our normal route home. We quickened our steps, but try as we might, we couldn't widen the gap between the bully and us. My friend finally broke into a dead run, but I couldn't because of Fred. He was a bit fragile and needed some extra attention to stay in one piece.

The bully quickly reached my side, and immediately the torment started. My books ended up on the street, but somehow I managed to keep Fred from the bully's grasp. My mini triumph at keeping Fred safe was short lived as the bully grabbed my wrist and started to twist. Neither shrieking in pain nor shouting "uncle" would satisfy my tormentor—he wanted Fred and made his demand clearly known. Reluctantly I gave Fred over and dropped to the ground when I was released from the death grasp.

From the ground, I pleaded for Fred's life as my friend looked on from a safe distance. I begged for the bully to give Fred back, since he was expected at Thanksgiving dinner. Okay, I didn't personalize Fred to my tormentor, but it was important for me to get Fred (and his perfectly selected gumdrop feet) home. The bully just laughed at me and teasingly held Fred at arm's length as I tried in vain to snatch him away.

As the bully grew tired of his game—and as I was running out of tears to cry—he hit me with the fatal blow. He nonchalantly pulled Fred's feet from their toothpick legs, threw them to the ground, and stepped on them. I was crushed.

I'm not sure how it happened, but by the end of the encounter, feetless Fred was back in my possession. I gathered my scattered books, scraped Fred's feet off the pavement, and walked home, defeated.

When Mom got home from work, she listened intently as I retold my story, complete with another full set of tears. As mothers invariably do, Mom had a solution. She quickly replaced Fred's feet with two new gumdrops (lemon and lime). Standing a little crooked (the bullying had taken a bit out of him), Fred took his position at the center of the dining room table for the holiday.

For all the relatives who joined us that Thanksgiving, Fred was the center of attention (at least when it came to table centerpieces). He served the family and the feast proudly, but I knew Fred wasn't the turkey I had carried out of school just a few days earlier. He was lopsided and standing on lemon and lime feet—feet I did not pick out or want to be a part of Fred.

This incident stands out as the pivotal point when I had let someone else determine how I felt about myself. The bully, through his actions, had left me feeling a like failure. I could create a worthwhile project (Fred), but I was not equipped to manage it to completion (display a cherry and grape footed Fred as our Thanksgiving centerpiece).

After joining the corporate workforce years later, ensuring I had the right "gumdrops" in the right place continued to significantly influence my work habits. Working with others, I held on a little too tightly to the design and direction of a collaborative effort, at times squashing others' creativity. I played it 'safe' by not getting involved in efforts where I could not control the outcome. I obsessed about meeting project objectives and implementation delivery efforts, to the detriment of other aspects of my life. Foregoing family obligations, exercise and social engagements to focus my attention on the project was a regular occurrence. I received accolades for my accomplishments at the office, but was left woefully out of balance in life.

Distinguishing how an event so far in my past was shaping my present actions was not easy. However once I did, I could choose something different. I gradually began to collaborate more on work efforts, allowing the creativity of others into the process. I created a better balance to my life by ensuring my personal well being and relationships had their appropriate priority. Life didn't change overnight, but today my life is more productive and personally fulfilling than my previous actions would have led me to, had I allowed the bully to continue to steal my gumdrops (influence my actions).

GETTING NAKED

1. When in your life have you changed your routine, only to have something bad happen that left you saying "I

should have. . ." or "If only I had. . ." or "I will never do that again"? For each incident, what have you given up in order to stay "safe"? Are you still playing it safe?

2. When has your life's "bully" taken you away from a task, an idea, or a person that inspired you, energized you, or made you happy? Is your bully still haunting you?

3. Where in your life are you giving away your power, enthusiasm, and passion to someone or something? What are you giving away and to whom or what? How long will you allow this to continue?

4. Where in your life have you focused on one aspect of a project, an idea, or your life so intently that you are now lopsided? For each incident, are you willing to give up focusing on your "gumdrop" in order to restore balance? Why or why not?

CHAPTER 5

EVERYONE HAS THEIR OWN CRAP

I recently read a quote attributed to 17th century English author Owen Feltham: "The greatest results in life are usually attained by simple means and the exercise of ordinary qualities. These may for the most part be summed up in these two: common-sense and perseverance." The message I got from this quote is that we're all capable of overcoming crises and achieving greatness. Hmm—this is challenging, since I don't always feel capable of these things; in fact, I often feel somewhat small and insignificant. I'll step out on a limb and say that many of you could say the same thing about yourself. But we're all capable of doing amazing things, no matter what challenges we have to deal with along the way.

My dad's wife once made the comment that "everyone has their own crap" to deal with. Now in her case, it was a mother-in-law who was exceptionally demanding and highly critical and who didn't hesitate to tell you exactly what she thought (usually negative). You may have worked for years to overcome controlling or overprotective parents, unrealistic expectations, in-law issues, your own self-defeating or self-limiting behaviors, or whatever your particular challenge is. We all have situations in our lives that we need to deal with, whether they are dysfunctional families, relationship issues, health concerns, career and business problems, or our own personal demons.

Picture these aspects of your life as a messy room or closet in your house. It's full of accumulated stuff from your past—lots of it may be junk, some of it reminds you of painful memories, and a few treasured items are mixed in. Taking time to clean out that room or closet is refreshing and opens up that space for uses you really value. It's the same with your life. By taking the time to really deal with those personal issues, past struggles, or painful memories, you actually open up space within yourself to let happier and more positive experiences in.

Several years ago, a close friend discovered that her business partner was taking money from the business to pay personal expenses. When she confronted her business partner about this, she was met with denial that escalated into a physical altercation in which my friend's shoulder was seriously injured. For years afterward, she held on to this memory as a reminder not to let herself get into a situation like that again. Every time her shoulder ached, she thought of the incident. And every time she opened her closet and saw the oversized white shirt she had been wearing that day, she was reminded not to let her guard down. One day I got an email from her saying she was getting rid of the white shirt. She had realized that she needed to let go of the memory and that she couldn't do that without getting rid of the shirt. She knew that as long as she kept hanging on to this memory, she wasn't trusting that she had learned from the past. By not trusting herself, she was staying small and less impactful in the rest of her life. How's that for an extraordinary insight? For you and I the lesson here is just because we all have crap doesn't mean we should hang on to it. We have to know when to let go.

Another woman I worked with lost her husband very suddenly. One day he was perfectly healthy; the next day he was undergoing emergency surgery, only to learn he had incurable cancer. He passed away within a week. Talk about a shock! Before Barb knew what had happened, she was a single parent raising three kids, ages ten, seven, and one. Besides dealing with her own grief, she also had to help her children understand why their dad wouldn't be coming home.

At the time her husband died, Barb had a successful career in human resources, so she'd seen plenty of people go through similar crises—she just never thought it would be her. She stayed at home for a short time, but realized she had to keep moving forward, for the kids if not for herself. She soon found a passion for fundraising through LIVESTRONG (the foundation founded by cancer survivor and champion cyclist Lance Armstrong), which allows her to continue her journey through grief while also giving back.

Over time, Barb has started dating again. She took a management job in the life insurance industry and is a spokesperson for the benefits of life insurance for families. She leans on friends and family for support when times get tough and would be the first to say she doesn't always have the answers or make the best decisions. Despite all the "crap" life has handed her, she continues to put one foot in front of the other and is determined to get up and live each day to the fullest—not hide and pull the covers over her head.

Let me tell you about David. David grew up in a home with little praise, encouragement, or nurturing. His father was extremely tough on him—physical discipline was frequent and verbal put-downs the norm. To escape, David joined the Air Force and later started a family, determined to create the type of family life he never had. When his son was diagnosed with autism, David and his wife were devastated. As a father, he talked about the lost dreams of enjoying ball games with his son and sharing his love of airplanes. He started to doubt his ability to build a better life for his family than he had experienced.

Eventually David started a sports league for autistic children in his community. It became so successful that it was featured on several local TV stations and hundreds of children have benefitted. David found a way to draw on his own experiences and his desire to create the best life possible for his son and ended up having an impact beyond anything he could have imagined.

Your story might not be this dramatic, or it might be more so. The point is that each of us has aspects of our life that we wish had been different or just hadn't happened at all. The key is to keep moving forward instead of getting stuck in "what ifs" and "if onlys". Sometimes you find strength or abilities you never knew you had.

So I go back to the quote that opened this chapter—I guess ordinary people like you and me really <u>can</u> do some amazing things.

GETTING NAKED

1. What "big white shirts" are you still holding on to? How would it feel to get rid of them? What new possibilities might open up to you?

2. Sometimes we're hesitant to really look at those parts of our lives that are most painful or difficult, thinking that if we could forget them, we'd be better off. Consider the thought that taking some time to face that period head on, rather than simply ignoring it, might help you really get past it. Take a few minutes to recall a painful or especially challenging part of your life. What made it difficult? What did you do to move beyond this incident? What did you learn from that situation? How has going through that situation helped you make different choices or decisions today?

2. What strategies do you have for relieving stress and to unwind? What can you do to keep yourself from "running

on empty"—spending so much time and energy on solving problems and dealing with issues (your own or those of others) that you have nothing left in the tank for yourself?

3. It's easy to get so in the mode of dealing with problems and "fixing" things that you forget to have fun. What have you done for fun today? This week? This month? Plan some five- to ten-minute fun breaks during your day. Be specific about how you will spend this 'fun' time— you deserve it!

CHAPTER 6

ISLAND LIVING

Intelligent, talented, confident, strong, successful, hard worker, results-oriented. Do any of these words describe you? Many of us have spent our careers honing these qualities and building a strong reputation based on this foundation. Unfortunately, another word may also describe you, if you're willing to admit it: isolated.

I don't mean you are a social outcast, have no friends, or don't work well with your coworkers or those you lead. Likely the opposite is true. You probably have friends and family you enjoy spending time with, and your coworkers would say you have strong relationship skills. But despite this, you can tend to keep people at arm's length. You may be friendly and enjoy lively conversations, yet rarely share anything meaningful about yourself or let people see the "real" you. Maybe your conversations rarely go beyond "Hi, how are you?" or "How was your weekend?" You may even tend to hang back when the group goes to lunch together or plans an after work social event, often with the excuse that you have "too much to do".

The mental picture of this phenomenon for me is a remote desert island. The island I'm talking about is not a physical location you travel to, it exists right where you live and if you move, it moves with you. This island is deserted, one small mound of sand surrounded by water. You sit under the one lone palm tree, which offers little shade, in the middle of your island.

It's easy to get lulled into living with a sense of solitude by not really opening ourselves up to the people in our lives. Too often it's easier to jump to the role of helper, advisor, leader, giver, or super-parent, and deflect others' attempts to get to know us. We don't experience the lightened load that true friendship or closeness with others offers us. Desert island living offers us protection from being hurt, criticized, or taken advantage of, but we also miss out on the joy of sharing life's ups and downs with others. We can truly feel "alone in a crowd".

Let me illustrate using a couple of examples of real people, starting with myself. During my career in the corporate world I have usually been in a leadership role of some type, responsible for guiding, mentoring and coaching others. Since I'm an introvert by nature, all this outflow of energy leaves me drained at the end of the day or week, so I attempt to refresh myself and renew my energy with alone time—going for a walk, exercising in my home gym, working in the yard, writing. While this provides me with some needed balance, it also reinforces my tendency to remain on my island and deflect others' attempts to get to know me.

Even when a family member or close friend asks me a serious question about my career or relationship I may avoid answering by saying something vague or philosophical in response. I am quite good at finding a way to shift the topic if it becomes uncomfortable or I don't want to reveal what really matters to me. I am much more comfortable internalizing my thoughts and feelings rather than speaking openly about them. Unfortunately, the result is conversations don't get below the surface and I'm often left with a vague feeling of emptiness and aloneness.

Maybe your personality is more like my friend Jackie's— outgoing, positive, never at a loss for casual conversation or a funny story. She actually thrives on interacting with a wide variety of people and is always planning some type of social event or activity to bring people together. She is continually driven to do more, experience more, and spend more time with others. This high-achieving woman never stops! However, she's so focused on the next thing to do or keeping conversations light and entertaining that she has honed her own deflection skills. She can skillfully shift a topic from one of greater importance to one of relative unimportance by telling a story from the latest reality show or movie. For friends, family, and others trying to penetrate the wall of a deflector, this "skill" provides a pretty significant challenge since open and honest communication is a major building block for relationships both in social and professional circles.

There are several strategies that can help you move past your own deflection habit and get more comfortable with deeper, open communication:

1. Recognize the deflection for what it is – a way to avoid the question being asked or to let others see the real you.

2. Identify the top one or two topics that you tend to avoid like the plague and the deflection techniques you use (e.g. humor, shifting the question, making excuses, etc.).

3. The next time a close friend, family member or some-one else you trust brings up one of these topics, be aware of your deflection reflex and respond as directly as possible. Remember that this person is not there to hurt you.

4. Remember that you are not being graded on your answer. Share what you feel comfortable sharing plus a little more. This will help you expand your comfort zone in opening yourself to others.

I believe that each one of us was created with a need to connect to another person that we can be real with. This might be a spouse or partner, a best friend, a mentor, a family member, or a combination of these and others. These types of relationships allow us to interact, be vulnerable, and find better solutions together than we could find on our own. They force us to see ourselves for who we really are and be okay with that. You may even find, like I have, that it gives you a stronger sense of self that allows you to be more authentic (the real you!) to those you work with.

GETTING NAKED

1. Imagine connecting with someone on a level where there is equal give and take in the relationship, where you let them see the real you—warts and all, where there is deep listening with no judgment, advice with no strings, just real caring and wanting what's best for each other. How would this make you feel?

2. How would you benefit in your work by being able to let someone into your life—to really build rapport? How would your personal life benefit?

3. If moving beyond being a leader, advisor, fixer, giver, etc. to another person feels threatening or scary to you, can you pinpoint why? (Are you worried that people will see you as weak, that they won't like the "real" you, that you need to maintain a certain image?) Whatever scenario you have in your head, try playing it out. For example, how would you know people are seeing you as weak? What would they do or say? Who specifically would do this? Would they really? If they did, how would that change who you are?

4. Connections are important in many aspects of our lives:

- With people who energize you—remember that we all need relationships that give something to us, not just put us in the role of giver.

- With work you enjoy—doing something you are passionate about and gets you excited to get up every day.

- With real life—home is where the people whom you care about and who care about you are. This is what's real—not some dream home, dream job, or dream city.

- With who you are and choose to be—not reacting based on old baggage. It's your life story to write, so how do you want your story to go from here?

Do any of these resonate with you? How can you start this week to build the types of connections you want and need?

5. How would being more authentic—more your real self—with those your work with impact your leadership? Your role as a peer? Your ability to influence others?

CHAPTER 7

THE CONNECTION GAME

Now that you have gotten off your island and are aware of any tendency to deflect others' attempts at deeper conversation, it's a great time to look at how to initiate a connection with others.

Attending a seminar recently, I came across a glimpse of my former self, and it took me back to a key lesson I learned a few years ago. First, let me tell you about the meeting planner I came in contact with: focused on her tasks, dressed for the role, moving through the group ensuring that everything was running as planned. Attached to a headset and a constant look of concern on her face, she walked with purpose from task to task. Her eyes remained focused on her clipboard; speaking to others only to give commands or get needed information. To no participant's surprise, the meeting was going off without a hitch. However, since there was a team of people available to help manage the meeting, I was left thinking that this person was missing a prime opportunity to connect with her peers and the leaders of her organization.

Seeing this behavior in another person took me back to the days when I acted similarly. I walked quickly between meetings, head down, deep in thought about the meeting I had just left, the one I was heading to, or the tasks awaiting me at my desk. I didn't acknowledge people I passed. I was missing out on multiple opportunities to say hello to those I worked with, to learn more about what was happening in my company—and at a very basic level to connect, even for a moment, with another human being.

Although I lean more toward being an introvert than an extrovert, I have never considered myself antisocial, and those who know me would laugh heartily at such a descriptor. However, working with a mentor one day, I became acutely aware of the potential cost of my "hallway" habit. It became crystal clear that others who don't know me might consider me antisocial or worse: "She's all work and no play." "Does she ever smile?" "She's so one-dimensional." "She can't possibly relate to me."

In discussing my habit with my similarly introverted mentor, he offered up his secret of how to be more of an extrovert when others are present, thus connecting with them on some level. It's all about putting on your extrovert "game face" with a simple three-step process: smile, make eye contact, and greet people you pass.

Believe it or not—and those who connect easily with others in their personal life may find it hard to believe—this process may take some practice in the workplace at first. For me, it seemed like I was cheating the company, because I didn't feel this activity aligned with my dedication to the job. However, I was willing to see what being outside my comfort zone might offer, knowing I could always revert to my previous method if needed.

I started out with sticky notes in my car and at my desk to remind me of the three-step process. Although I didn't succeed very often those first few days, I kept at it. I made a game of walking around with a smile on my face, looking others in the eye, and saying hello. Eventually I started to sense a change in me and those I came in contact with, and I learned a few things in the process.

I learned that most people don't smile first thing in the morning and are suspicious of anyone who does. I learned that most people will say hello to you if you say it first. I learned the gift of making eye contact with others and seeing their "hello" smile spread to their eyes. What a treat!

The best lesson I took away from this experience, however, was that I became a more productive employee. I arrived at my desk and meetings with a certain lightness about me, ready to work. In the eyes of others, I became approachable, a team player, a person whose ideas warranted listening to. In the end, what started out as a game of connection has become a part of who I am today and how I interact with others. Most importantly, it has allowed me to become the contributor to my company I have always wanted to be.

GETTING NAKED

1. Visualize the meeting planner's behavior described in the first two paragraphs. Have you ever crossed paths with a "focused" employee like this? What were your first impressions of this person?

2. Did you have the opportunity to get to know this "focused" employee? What was this person like once you got to know them? Was this consistent with your first impression? Have you shared these experiences with this person? Will you? Why or why not?

3. If you are the "focused" employee, what are some first impressions others have shared with you? Are these impressions consistent with who you know yourself to be? If not, what will you do differently?

4. What is your "connection game" you play with coworkers, company associates, and strangers?

5. If you don't have a way of connecting with others, are you willing to try something new to see what is possible? Describe the connection game you will play.

6. Play your connection game. Jot down a few of your findings and share them with someone.

CHAPTER 8

CREATING MEMORIES

In the previous chapter we examined the benefits of being aware of how others perceive you and learning to get out of your own head in order to connect with the people around you. Now let's take that a step further and look at the kind of relationships and experiences that build shared memories.

Boat people. You either are one or you're not. Boat people speak a special language that includes words like bow, stern, starboard, fenders, and impellers. They spend a lot of time talking to other boat people about the best places to go boating, wind conditions, and the cost of repairs (there's always something to repair on a boat, it seems). They usually grew up in a boating family and have childhood memories of water-skiing, tubing, and long days on the water.

I am not a boat person. I've never been on water skis, can't tie any of those special knots, and don't know how to "tie up" or how boat lifts work. I've never driven a boat and don't have a clue about the rules of the water and the confusing language of buoys (how do you even pronounce that word?). My childhood memories of boats are mainly bumper boats found in the local amusement park.

My mom and I once tried to create a special mother-daughter memory by going tandem kayaking. After we got out to the middle of the small lake, we were so tired that we could only go in circles. We started laughing so hard at our inability to make progress that pretty soon all we could do was sit there weakly until someone hauled us back to shore. Another time, my partner took me out on a small sailboat to show me the skills she had mastered growing up on the Jersey shore in a boating family. Just as we got going and I was starting to enjoy myself, we ran into a sandbar, stopping dead and giving me a case of whiplash that I still won't let her forget.

On a recent beautiful fall day, I went with my best friend (a boat person) to move her boat to its new home in another part of Lake of the Ozarks, Missouri. The trip was going to take a couple of hours by water, and we were looking forward to a relaxing boat ride, enjoying the water and chatting.

About ten minutes into the trip, something didn't sound right. When we opened the hatch to the engine compartment, we saw that water was rushing in and the bilge pump, which was supposed to pump water out of the compartment, wasn't working. As the boat got lower and lower in the water, we tried to find a boat lift nearby, to no avail. By now water was spewing like a fountain from the engine compartment.

I started bailing, as I was being blasted in the face with the fountain of oily water, while my friend shouted instructions (boat people like to do that) and steered us back to our dock. Somehow we made it back—barely—and got the boat safely on the lift. It took us another couple of exhausting hours to get the water out. By the time we were done, we were covered in dirty water, oil, and sweat. Thank goodness no pictures exist of that moment! Suffice it to say that a shower and many margaritas later, we were nearly good as new.

Okay, so I'm still not a boat person, but I learned something from these adventures. First, boat people need to have a sense of humor. Whether spinning in circles, hitting a sandbar or being covered in oily water, all of these experiences are funny now. Second, boating adventures create a special memory and bond between the people involved. They give us the chance to laugh about the situation and at ourselves, shake our heads in wonder, and draw closer as we retell (often with embellishment) the stories.

In a work context, these stories remind me of the importance of enjoying the people around me, being intentional about creating memories, and not moving so quickly to the next thing to do. This is hard for someone hardwired to be a fixer, problem solver, and doer. It's not that I mean to leave out the people around me, but sometimes I get so focused on achieving the desired result or moving on to the next "to do" that I fail to build the rapport that is so essential to both work and personal relationships. It's rapport that gives us the ability to understand someone else's viewpoint or relate to someone else's feelings...that sense of being on the same wavelength.

For me, there are three keys to building the type of rapport that results in shared memories: ask questions – laugh – be intentional. I start out by asking questions about someone's interests, family, job, and so on. Then I really listen to what the person has to say. This typically leads to the opportunity to share something about myself as well. It amazes me how often there is something we have in common that begins to develop into a connection or bond between us. Second, I try to look for opportunities to share a laugh with others. Whether it's over something on TV or your boss's latest foible, a good laugh makes us feel more alive and connected with each other. It also lowers our stress level and who doesn't need that? Finally, memories don't just happen you have to be intentional about making them. Take time to go to lunch with your coworkers once in awhile or share a laugh during a coffee break. Go on vacation and don't take your smart phone. Do you want your kids, spouse and coworkers to remember you as "all work and no play"?

I find that when I build this type of rapport with others, it's so much easier to openly share ideas, assume the best of each other, and work together to achieve business goals. This can mean the difference between a ho-hum workplace and a dynamic, positive work environment where teamwork grows and strong relationships thrive.

GETTING NAKED

1. What do you have in common with those you work with—experiences, traits, ideas, interests, values?

2. Whom, specifically, do you need to get to know better? What questions can you use to help draw that person out? What can you share about yourself?

3. What stories do you love to retell with family and friends? What is it about these stories that you enjoy remembering?

4. What have you done lately to break from your normal routine and increase your odds of creating a memorable time to look back on? With your kids you could build a snowman or create a new recipe together. With a significant other or friends you might take a dance class or take up disc golf. At work, try letting go and being spontaneous. When coworkers ask you to go out for lunch, resist the urge to say you're too busy and go! Remember that tomorrow's memories start today.

CHAPTER 9

SETTING BOUNDARIES WITH OTHERS

Pick a game, any game. The one thing you can count on is that the game has rules by which to play or boundaries inside of which you must stay. Baseball has foul lines and base paths, football has sidelines and end zones, golf has out-of-bounds areas, and the card game spades has rules specifying how trump is determined and which card is higher or has more power than another. Give me a game any day! It's nice to know what the boundaries and rules are before you begin to play.

Here's a tip for you—relationships, whether in the workplace or not, also have boundaries. A boundary can be as simple as to get a timely response, send me an email versus leave a voicemail. Boundaries which are a little harder to discern may sound like this: When I share my opinion in a private conversation, you are not to repeat this information without my permission. Unfortunately, relationships don't come with a rule book like games do. Thus, boundaries are rarely communicated before a relationship begins. We merrily engage in a relationship until someone violates an unspoken boundary, resulting in anger, hurt feelings or mistrust on one side and perhaps bewilderment, confusion, etc. on the other.

If boundaries and rules were known before relationships ever began, think of the difference this would make in our world! There would be lower employee turnover, fewer employee performance issues, fewer family feuds, lower divorce rates. . . the list goes on and on.

Even when boundaries have been shared, they may not be clearly understood. One person may think that she clearly set limits, but her comments might not have registered as a boundary to the other person. Or the listener may believe he heard a boundary being set, while the speaker wasn't thinking of his comments that way at all. Let's face it—very few people ask to have a conversation about relationship boundaries *and* test for clarity that what was shared was understood just the way it was intended. In some cases, by the time spoken boundaries become thoroughly understood, too much damage has already occurred and the relationship cannot be salvaged. Hindsight tells us there is value in making sure any boundary is clearly stated so that all relationship participants understand it.

Through much of my adolescence and young adult years, I was my mom's confidante—she regularly shared details of her marital and financial issues with me and looked for me to offer advice or a sympathetic ear. But at some point, those conversations started leaving me feeling drained, frustrated, and angry. I realized they were no longer making me feel closer to my mother; now they were an invasion of my "personal space" and were occurring without my permission or desire. I began avoiding family events and often would snap at whoever I happened to talk to after a conversation with my mother. It became apparent that I needed to establish some boundaries for my own well-being and so I could be comfortable spending time with my mother.

Setting boundaries in your relationships is easier if you say something the moment someone else's words or actions make you uncomfortable. You know what that moment feels like—you sit up a little straighter, maybe slightly cock your head and raise an eyebrow, or a tingle shoots through your body. This is the moment when setting a needed boundary will be most effective. The sooner you can set the boundary, the less likely negative emotions, such as anger and frustration, will build up within you and set off emotional fireworks. Instead, establishing the boundary becomes just another topic in your conversation.

In my case, the beginning of my discomfort with my mother was in the distant past, so taking action right away was no longer an option. But I could still do something. Whether you address the problem right away or at a later time, the steps in setting boundaries remain the same:

1. Create a safe space to have the conversation. Make sure your audience is focused on your discussion, not texting, cleaning the kitchen, or taking care of the kids.

2. Make it known you are talking about a certain behavior, not the person as a whole. Explain that you are interested

in setting a boundary in your relationship, not changing who the person is.

3. Be vulnerable. Tell the person how the behavior in question makes you feel—but do so calmly, without dumping built-up emotions on them.

4. Ask for what you need. Be clear and matter of fact.

5. Ask your audience to repeat back what they heard you say. Then, if needed, clarify your intentions.

6. Negotiate for the boundary. This step may take some time as you work to get on the same page regarding a boundary that both of you (or all of you, if it's a group) can agree on.

7. Be firm. Hold yourself accountable to the boundary you created, and hold others accountable as well. This is the one area most people fall down in. But why go through all the trouble of setting a boundary if you're just going to end up where you started because you don't stick to it?

Setting a boundary is not typically a "one and done" type of event, especially if the behavior you have set a boundary around has been in existence for awhile. As for my mother and me, it took some time for us to "get there." Asking for and getting agreement from my mother that we not talk about her marriage or financial issues was relatively easy. Where we struggled was being firm with each other to steer clear of these topics when we talked. Occasionally one or the other of us would fall into old habits, but we shared the responsibility to hold each other accountable to our boundary and could get the conversation back on track very quickly. In the end, we have created a much healthier, more enjoyable relationship than we would have had without the life-altering boundary conversation.

GETTING NAKED

1. Do you have some relationships that leave you frustrated, angry, or de-energized? If so, with whom? What emotion are you left feeling and why? (Be sure to include your work relationships.)

2. Do these negative emotions spill over into relationships you have with others? If so, how?

3. Do you need to set boundaries in any of these relationships? If so, for each relationship, identify the boundary that is needed.

4. Are you willing to have the needed conversations? If so, review the six steps above. For each boundary desired, identify the behavior, how it makes you feel, and what you need.

5. Set a date by which you will have the needed conversations. This is good practice for holding yourself accountable. If needed, share these dates with someone else and ask them to hold you accountable.

6. After the boundary is agreed to, check in with yourself periodically. How do you feel about the relationship now? Do you need to tweak the boundary you established? Are you holding yourself and your relationship partner(s) accountable to the boundary?

7. Reward yourself! You are well on your way to creating relationships that empower you to be the best you can be for everyone in your life!

CHAPTER 10

You Deserve a Life You Love

Ever have one of those coworkers that you are simply in awe of? The person who seems to have it all together? This person is head and shoulders above her peer group, not only managing her own workload, but doing the extra work (cheerleading, coaching, executing) to ensure the whole department runs smoothly. This person is respected by staff, peers, and leadership and works tirelessly, with a positive, engaging personality. Sounds too good to be true, doesn't it?

I have had the pleasure of working with such a person as a peer. I simply marveled at what she could accomplish while staying connected to the people who surrounded her, striking the perfect balance between in-office banter and strategic, work-related dialogue. I was excited when we were asked to work together on a department project. Over the course of this assignment we became friends, discussing work and life issues as I never had with any other coworker in my career.

I learned that my friend had helped her mother through some financial issues, even bringing her mother to live with her for nearly a year. I learned she was in a twenty-year-plus relationship with someone who in the last several years had been battling (or more accurately, ignoring) a diagnosis of depression. I learned she was working through the impact of an unwanted transfer within our company. All this, and she still brought her "A-game" to work daily! No one would know that these large life issues were weighing on her mind as she worked through each day. She was our department's go-to person.

One afternoon, my friend found the courage to verbalize her reasoning for these actions, and it was then I learned the real lesson. We were sitting in a break room discussing the day's happenings, when out of the blue she said, "Do you want to know why I take on everything I take on? I feel like if I do X, I will earn Y. If I help my mom, I will earn more of my family's love and respect. If I allow my partner to treat her disease in her own way, I will earn the relationship I want. If I accept this transfer graciously, I will earn a role equal to my talents."

Wow! What a revelation about someone who was Wonder Woman to those around her. We talked about how this cycle led to a lot of accomplishments on her life's to-do list. But then I asked her how she felt about her accomplishments, and her eyes welled with tears. She said, "I feel tired. There always has been and always will be something else to do."

At that moment, I was looking at the loneliest person in the world, and my heart went out to her. My friend was caught in a trap. Not the kind of trap where steel claws crush an ankle, causing severe pain when they close. This was a trap she couldn't see, but in some ways it was just as painful. The problem with this "action/reward" trap is the only person who can get you out of this trap is the person that is in it. Not caught in her trap, I quickly distinguished her energy draining, never ending cycle of to do's for wanted rewards. However, she needed to recognize there would always be the next X to do and Y to earn, if she continued to make her choices from that framework. And until she recognized this and dealt with how she made her choices, she would never escape her trap.

As our conversation continued, I shared some advice about finding a more empowering way to live life. I said, "Doing things in order to earn something is definitely one way to go through life, but I choose to believe something else for you. Knowing you the way I do, I think you would've helped your mother, been there for your partner, and made the most of this transfer, regardless of the possibility of earning a reward. Is this true?" She nodded in agreement. "So whether or not you 'earn' the goals you seek, I choose to believe you deserve a life that you love." She looked at me in surprise. "It doesn't mean there isn't work associated with having a life that you love. You have to stay conscious to the decisions you make to ensure you are choosing the life you want instead of doing what you think will earn your next reward. This doesn't necessarily mean your decisions will be different. It means each decision is your choice and the reward you are seeking comes in owning, and then powerfully living, your choices."

This was definitely a life learning moment. I saw so much of my life pass before my eyes—times when I too had chosen to do what I thought would earn my next reward. If I continuously take on extra assignments at work, I will get promoted. But the reality of this choice is I take on extra work because I love to be challenged and learn something new. Instead of going on the annual family vacation to be recognized as a wonderful daughter, I chose to go on the trips to hang out with my parents, brother, sister and their kids.

Our conversation became an "ah-ha" moment for my friend as well. She looked at her choices differently. She knew she would've done anything to help her mother regardless of how other family members perceived her actions. She took responsibility for her decision to transfer with her company, knowing this move put her in the best position to pursue other career opportunities with her current employer. As for her relationship, my friend chose to speak up (see Chapter 12 – Finding Your Voice). She set boundaries (see Chapter 9) and a timetable for action by her partner to manage her illness. Her actions helped create the relationship she always wanted and now enjoys.

GETTING NAKED

1. Are you living your life caught in a trap? Is there a part of your life that leaves you tired and without energy? If so, what is the trap?

2. Are you living a life that you love? If so, do you "own" that you deserve this life? How?

3. If you aren't living a life that you love, are you willing to consciously make choices to create that life? What would those choices be?

4. Are you worth the effort? If so, why? If you don't believe you are worth the effort, why not?

CHAPTER 11

CHOOSING YOUR LIFE

J ust think about the number of people you know, at work or in your personal life, who have said at one time or another, "I don't really enjoy what I do for a living," "I want to spend more time doing X," or "I need to spend more time with the people who are most important to me." I've said all of these and more at different points in my life. And I've talked myself out of doing what I really want to do more times than I can remember—all with good reason, of course. "I need this job to secure my future." "Yes, I want to do X, but I need to spend time doing Y." "I can't spend the time I need to with certain people because I also want to spend time with my partner, and mixing the two drains me."

Pretty lame, right? I've known for years that everything is a choice, so why did I stop choosing? Well, I didn't stop choosing. I stopped taking responsibility for my choices and instead chose to just let life happen to me. What I was left with was unfulfilled expectations, failure to reach goals, inner frustration, and loss of contact with those inspirational, unconditionally loving people who energize me. Not an enjoyable way to go through the days, let me tell you.

The switch from choosing your life to just letting it happen is very subtle—so subtle that you may not even recognize that it is happening, or worse yet, that it has already occurred. This is a danger that anyone can fall victim to.

My career followed a pattern that may sound familiar to you: go to college, interview, accept a position (even though you have no idea what the job really entails), and start working. Once in the position, figure out what you *really* want to do. Then either stay in the role, leave the company, or, if the company is big enough, move around within the organization.

I chose the latter and began my journey through different departments and work challenges within my company. I was fortunate to have a variety of opportunities, with accolades for the results I generated and growth experiences to mold me into a more complete employee. However, I started to hear more and more frequently that in order to be considered for promotion, I needed more experience in the company's core business, or in leading a large number of people, or in a particular skill set.

This is when I started to let my professional life happen to me. I chased the experiences my management said I needed instead of really taking an honest look at myself and these "opportunities" to determine whether each one was what I was really interested in doing.

It took numerous experiences over several years for me to get clarity around this. I went through periods of grieving (why did I leave that position?), anger (why isn't the company taking better care of such a high-performing employee as me?), and settling (I guess I'm not as good as I thought I was or as others led me to believe). None of these emotions were comforting, yet I kept moving through them, revisiting each multiple times. Finally I got tired of my own thoughts and decided to start making decisions and taking action.

Here are the steps I found most helpful in clarifying my career direction:

1. Identify your technical and people skills. This may take some time. Talk with coworkers, people you worked for over the years, and mentors to gather their perceptions, compare this to your perception of yourself and make an honest evaluation.

   Note: It is important to identify your strongest skills, as I found in my varied experiences, I could do many things; however, I wasn't always tapping into my strengths.

2. Identify the types of work you like to do. If you're going to spend a third or more of each weekday at work it's key to like what you do.

3. Explore roles within your company that align with your skills and interests. Talk to your employee services office or a mentor about possible roles that match your skills and interests. Talk to someone who is doing a job you are interested in to understand the various aspects of the role. Search your company's employee websites for information.

4. Talk with your management or a mentor about your skills and interests and how your company would benefit from you being in roles that align with them. By focusing on how your company benefits from matching your skills and interest to a role you demonstrate your commitment to your employer even though you may, at some point, leave your current role.

5. Update your résumé and keep it updated. This activity keeps you focused on matching your skills and interests to opportunities. You may never use your résumé to find other employment; however, having your résumé up to date keeps this option readily available should you need or want to.

By taking these steps, I actively chose and continue to choose my work life instead of being a victim to whatever someone else says I'm good enough to do. I have used a similar methodology to choose how and with whom I will spend my personal time from day to day, month to month, and year to year. Calling it a methodology may sound somewhat cold, but this is not my intent. My goal is to establish actionable steps that keep me engaged in choosing my life rather than just going along for the ride. I want to experience life, not have a life full of experiences that don't resonate with my core values and leave me tired and empty.

If you feel the same way, here are five steps that can help you make your own choices in relationships:

1. Identify your core values—your physical, emotional, and spiritual foundation. These things are as vital to you as eating and breathing. They energize you.

2. Identify your strengths for your primary relationship, family relationships, and friends. What do you contribute to these relationships, regardless of the circumstances? If you are struggling with this task, start with a work relationship and identify your strengths for this relationship. Once you get started, identifying your personal life strengths may come a bit easier to you.

3. Identify your wants—the things you don't necessarily need in your life to be fulfilled, but that will enrich you. What activities do you like to do and with whom? What personality traits do you want to surround yourself with?

4. Identify your boundaries (see Chapter 9). Define the amount of time and effort you are willing to give to relationships that don't inspire you.

5. Find your voice (see Chapter 12) and share the outcomes of these steps with those in your life. Tell your significant other, your family and your friends your core values, strengths, wants and boundaries. Most important, allow them time to react, especially if sharing your thoughts about yourself isn't a routine activity, and listen to what this circle of people has to say.

I found these steps very challenging, since I didn't want to take a "deep dive" into myself. However, the cost of not taking these steps—frustration, being unfulfilled, anger, low energy—was greater.

In completing this exercise, I have realized many benefits. I am actively engaged in choosing my life. I am now clear on what is foundationally necessary for me to be the best I can be. I know what I can be counted on to give to my relationships, as well as the boundaries I need to keep my peace of mind. By identifying my wants, I make better choices about how, where, and with whom I want to spend my time, allowing me to make the most of each experience. And although I still do some things that I don't really want to, I know I am choosing to do these things. In making my choice, I also know I will find time to treat myself to something from my want list. Lastly, by having conversations with those closest to me, I have been able to strengthen many relationships while also recognizing that some relationships had run their course or needed to change. I fully choose the relationships I now have, just how they are. In the end, my relationships are just as they should be, and this is very freeing!

Life can just happen to you, both personally and professionally. The question is, do you have the courage to choose your life?

GETTING NAKED

1. Are you choosing your professional life or just letting it happen to you? Explain.

2. Are you in charge of your career? If yes, what are your actionable steps? If not, are you willing to take responsibility for your career?

3. Identify the steps you will take to create a professional life that inspires and energizes you. For "extra credit," include a timeline that challenges you.

4. Are you choosing your personal life or just letting it happen to you? Explain.

5. Are you energized by the people around you? If yes, let these people know their importance to you. If not, are you willing to take steps necessary to surround yourself with people who inspire you?

6. Identify the steps you will take to create a personal life (relationships and activities) that inspire and energize you. For "extra credit," include a timeline that challenges you.

CHAPTER 12

FINDING YOUR VOICE

I once had the opportunity to hear Matthew Shepard's mother speak to a large group. Matthew was the young man in Wyoming who was severely beaten, tied to a fence, and left for dead by a couple of men who didn't like the fact that he was gay. His mom, Judy, has since become an advocate for gay rights. She and her husband founded the Matthew Shepard Foundation in memory of their son, to help bring an end to antigay violence and promote a greater understanding of gay issues.

Something Judy Shepard said that day struck me. She talked about how nervous she used to get about public speaking, because she always felt like everyone was judging her—her appearance, her speaking ability, what she said, and how she said it. This made her feel very small and ineffective and created a tremendous amount of pressure that she carried with her every time she spoke. One day when the pressure seemed especially intense, she suddenly realized that all she had to do was be herself—it didn't matter what others thought of her. Her lack of professional polish and her less-than-perfect speaking skills do not get in the way of her telling a compelling and emotional story that moves people to action. She spends at least half of each year speaking to college groups and large corporate audiences, lobbying politicians, and testifying at hearings.

This is an ordinary mom who loved her son, attended countless school activities, cheered him from the audience at community theater, and worried about him being away at college. She was a former stay-at-home mom and schoolteacher, naturally reserved and soft-spoken—just a regular woman and mother who enjoyed her quiet life. Because of the terrible tragedy of her son's death, she was thrust into the limelight under the worst possible circumstances. She found her voice—a voice she likely never knew she had—and felt compelled to speak out.

Judy Shepard found something that we all struggle to find: a sense of self-assurance and purpose that comes from inside and doesn't need the approval of others. If you're like many of us, your voice is just a whisper that you're straining to hear—drowned out by a chorus of voices telling you what your body, friendships, marriage, children, social status, or career should be like and on what timeline. These voices form the ubiquitous "they" that seem to make all the rules we live by. "They" may be your parents, teachers, the media, a spouse, friends, social norms, or maybe your own high expectations for yourself. It can be hard to quiet these "should" messages so you can clearly hear the whisper of your own voice.

For some of us, due to a life circumstance such as the tragedy Judy Shepard experienced, the whisper may become a shout we can't ignore. But for most of us, life is a journey of making choices—one at a time, trying one path and then another—and in the end knowing that our voices are that much stronger because of what we learned through those experiences.

A colleague of mine is a successful trainer and personal development coach for a large corporation. Whenever I see Steve, he exudes positivity and energy. Over the years he has trained or consulted with countless people at all levels, and they continue to seek out his guidance and refer others to him. Steve is also an award-winning public speaker and facilitator who could have made a very good living as a travelling speaker. However, he didn't want to spend so much time away from his wife, so he found a way to use his motivation and speaking skills in a corporate environment that allows him to be home most nights. He literally "found his voice" and made a choice to use it to help people develop toward their dreams.

Like Steve, we can all find ourselves needing to separate what "they" say from what we really want for our lives. It's tiring to carry around the expectations, shoulds and should-nots from the world around us. We spend too much time and energy trying to find our voice outside ourselves, the same way we'd look for a set of lost keys, rather than where it really lives – inside each of us. Don't let "them" convince you there is only one right way to do things, to look, to act, to feel, or to achieve, when that internal whisper is telling you something else.

GETTING NAKED

1. Write down two or three "should" messages you're battling. For each one, make some notes about whether the message is consistent with what you want and what makes you happy. What would you do today if you let go of your "shoulds"?

2. What are one or two defining moments in your life when you gained an exciting insight into yourself or learned a valuable lesson? They don't have to be huge things—some examples might be when you mastered a new skill, heard a motivational speaker, or experienced your first kiss.

3. Do you get your sense of assurance from inside yourself or outside? Explain.

4. What is the voice inside your head saying that you need to hear? What will you do with this message?

5. What do you want to be known for? What kind of person do you want others to think of you as? Are you living your life consistent with this? If so, how? If not, what are you going to do differently now?

6. Think of something you've always wanted to do, but haven't gotten around to yet—such as starting your own business, writing a book, losing twenty pounds, or volunteering in

your community. What's the story you tell yourself about why you haven't done it yet? What's one small step you can take toward your goal in the next couple of days?

CHAPTER 13

SHARING THE JOURNEY

In his book *See You at the Top*, Zig Ziglar[1] quotes one of his favorite sayings: "A lot of people have gone further than they thought they could because someone else thought they could." I really like this quote, because it points out how important it is to have someone in your life who really knows you and believes in you—more than you believe in yourself. This could be a spouse, family member, friend, life coach, spiritual guide, or mentor. These individuals help guide us through life, confront our fears, and cast aside our long-held beliefs about who we are and what we are capable of. Our world is filled with examples of these types of mentor-advisor relationships: Maya Angelou and Oprah Winfrey, Phil Jackson and Michael Jordan, and even Yoda and Luke Skywalker.

A journey of self-discovery may be the most difficult trip any of us embark on. It's easy to pass through life, just doing the next thing on your to-do list, without really taking the time to ask yourself the hard questions, to examine who you are today and who you want to be in the future. There's always another load of laundry, one more errand, kids to raise, careers to build, and relationships to nurture. Our lives are filled with email, text messages, tweets, Facebook friends, and a constant stream of information from twenty-four-hour news channels. Then to "get away from it all," we go on vacation and spend a week relaxing, only to return to the same hectic pace. We need someone in our lives to help us take the time to step outside of our day-to-day activities and examine who we are and where we're headed.

Several years ago I was fortunate to meet someone who quickly became a good friend and someone I could share my journey with. We found that not only did we approach our work similarly, but we also enjoyed talking with each other about non-work-related things. As we became more comfortable, our conversations became a place where we could ask each other the really hard personal questions, share our experiences and what we learned from them, and most important, be a safe sounding board for one another. It was understood between us that whatever was said was accepted at face value—no judgment, sacred cows, or untouchable topics. We have sure talked about some sensitive topics over the years as we've faced career and family challenges, worked through issues with our partners or spouses, and struggled to understand our place in the world.

The immeasurable benefit of the hours of conversations we've had and experiences we've shared is that we each get to see ourselves and our actions from another perspective, which can lead to different choices in the future. Sometimes just having a safe place to share the thoughts swimming around in your head is enough to get you unstuck from old patterns or limitations and able to see things more clearly.

Over the years I've also known several people who have worked with an executive coach or life coach. It wasn't until I learned that several top executives at my company had worked with a coach, and I saw some of the changes they were making in their personal and professional lives, that I was willing to try it myself. There is immeasurable value in working with someone who has no emotional baggage with you and no preconceived ideas about your motives, intentions, or character. An effective coach can help you discover where you are in life (personally or professionally) and where you want to be, and help you do the work to get there.

One of the most important lessons I learned during my coaching experience was to stop racing to the next thing to do or the next goal to achieve and take some time to enjoy where I am in my life right then. Since I tend to mentor other individuals who are doers or high achievers like me, this is a lesson I try to pass on to them as well.

Life coach Debbie Delgado[2] summed up this idea in a newsletter article titled "You Are Enough":

> It's ironic that we've just celebrated Halloween—a day when people everywhere wear disguises and "become" someone other than themselves. I now realize that many of us wear a mask almost every day. We're afraid to be our authentic, true selves,

and so we become whatever we think the people around us want us to be.

What I now know is that the only thing you have to be is you. You were created as divinely as every other person on this planet. And you were sent here with your own unique gifts, talents, and quirks. And there are people on this planet who are here to be served by you.

How will they ever find you if you're pretending to be someone else?

What would your life be like if you dropped your mask? How much more energy would you have? How much lighter and happier you would feel? How much easier would your life be?

Mentors, coaches and close friends all help us take off our masks and show our true selves. They believe in you so much that they cause you to believe in yourself. They are a valuable collaborative partner in your journey through your life, career, relationships, self-discovery and much more.

Personally, I may have gotten to some of the same choices I have made inside the 'safe' zones created in these relationships. However, sharing my life's journey with these allies made parts of my journey shorter and sweeter, as I saw myself through their eyes and opened myself to the guidance and input of someone who genuinely cared about my well-being and success.

GETTING NAKED

1. How do you react to the statement "You are enough"?

2. How effective are you at asking others the really "hard" questions and listening to the answers in a way that makes them feel safe to be real with you? Explain.

3. How comfortable are you at having the tables turned and you answer the "hard" questions? Explain.

4. Which of these qualities of a trusted advisor, mentor, or close friend do you have: able to talk about a wide range of topics (both personal and work-related), great listener, good at asking and answering probing questions, able to create a safe atmosphere for dialogue, nonjudgmental, willing to be real? What other qualities do you think are important?

5. Who have been your best mentors over the years and what have you learned from them?

6. Discuss the questions at the end of Debbie Delgado's newsletter article.

CHAPTER 14

CURVEBALLS AND SUCKER PUNCHES

It was a particularly hard-fought college football game; emotions were still running high after the underdog team came from behind to win. Players from the losing team were grudgingly congratulating their opponents, and the victorious players were celebrating a thrilling victory. This scenario plays out dozens of times across the country every Saturday during football season. However, on this particular Saturday, a player from the losing team sucker punched a player from the winning team—slugged him right in the jaw. The guy never saw it coming and fell to the ground, clueless as to what had just occurred.

Ever feel like you've been sucker punched—hit hard by an unexpected event that leaves you looking around trying to figure out what just happened? Life has a way of throwing a sucker punch right when you least expect it. It may come in the form of a lost job, being passed over for a promotion, a car that suddenly stops running, the diagnosis of a serious medical condition, the death of someone close, the breakup of a relationship, or any one of a thousand other things. Or maybe it's more of a curveball, when life takes a turn that you weren't quite prepared for—a job transfer moves you away from family, a child decides to go to college far from home, or retirement isn't what you thought it would be.

So how do you respond when life doesn't go the way you expect it to? Awhile back I received an email from close friends who were dealing with a sucker punch of their own—breast cancer. Here's how they described their response:

> We have a plaque in our home that says "Life isn't measured by the number of breaths that you take, but by the moments that take your breath away." We found it years ago in a store, stumbled accidentally into it, actually. We both thought it was a great way to think about life, so we bought it. We brought it home, hung it up, and smiled. "What a great saying!" we enthusiastically thought. At the time, we were equating this saying with only good times. We reminisced about those types of moments when your heart is so full and you feel so great, and then all of a sudden you are so happy that you absolutely cannot breathe. Hopefully, we all have had those moments.
>
> Last April, we found that those moments come in the not-so-good times too. Last April, we heard the news that Laurie had breast cancer. When those words were spoken,

when we actually heard them out loud, when my worst fear was realized, I can tell you that *that* is another moment that literally takes your breath away. It takes it so far away that you truly believe you will never breathe again. In many ways, I don't know that we have breathed the same again since.

We've held our breath as we anxiously awaited test results and doctor's examinations. We've been short of breath from this tiring journey and emotional roller coaster. We've had our breath taken away with scares and worries, pain and heartache. And just when you think that you will not, you cannot, there is absolutely no way that you will take another breath, God whispers His hope into you, right where you need it, right when you need it, and holds your tired body and gives you strength. And just as He has promised, you do begin to breathe again. . . .

So when we got the word, while I was moving directly into the fetal position, [Laurie] was moving on and moving forward. While I was replaying the words over and over in my mind, briefly paralyzed by the doctor's voice, Laurie was already standing up, actually standing stronger. While the tears rolled down my face and I could not utter one audible word, Laurie asked "Where do we go from here," already anxious to get on with her life. I knew right then that cancer was not going to get in her way. I also knew that I was really going to have to buck up.

You see, as faithful as I try to be and as hopeful as I want to be, I have two very good friends named "Anxiety" and "Worry." They're inconsiderate friends, because they tend to come for visits around 2 a.m. and stay until just before the alarm rings. They wake me up from a somewhat sound sleep, start the conversation off with a few "what ifs," throw in a couple of "uh-ohs," and when I'm completely wide-eyed, they follow up with the ever dreaded "Here's one you might not have thought of." No wonder I'm barely breathing!

But Laurie, she sleeps. She must remember what Victor Hugo so eloquently reminds us: God is awake. She goes to sleep and stays asleep, knowing she will do what she can do and God will take it from there. . . .

Cancer certainly has tried, but it has never once won. . . . And as we sit here today, knowing that the next test is not until May 4th, the one that will tell us that chemo did the trick, we sit here in what we call "our breathing room." It's the time between chemo and radiation, needle pricks and additional tests, doctor's visits and painful worries. It's the time that we are trying to enjoy, to breathe again, to live.

Let me share that this story has a happy ending. Laurie's cancer is in remission and the prognosis is very good, thank goodness! This couple is such a great example of learning to breathe during both good times and bad. They really live their lives and share rich, meaningful relationships with family, friends, neighbors, coworkers, and their four-legged companions. They've experienced the highest of highs and the lowest of lows without becoming cynical or hardened or afraid. They could have decided that life was just too difficult and withdrawn, and none of us would have blamed them. How many times have we seen people react to hard times by striking out at those close to them, looking for someone to blame or asking "Why me?"

Do you remember how we all reacted after 9/11? We recoiled in horror, stared at the TV in disbelief, searched frantically for loved ones, withdrew to our homes in fear, avoided crowded places, and asked "What did we do to deserve this?" Some even reacted in anger and vowed revenge. But slowly we became more resolute, more determined to continue living our lives, more confident to travel and to believe that "normal" would return. Really living means experiencing the best and worst life has to offer, taking chances, exposing yourself to sometimes getting hurt, and sharing your life with others.

What draws me to read this email over and over is the sense of putting one foot in front of the other, one step at a time, no matter how difficult the situation. Laurie and her partner may not have known what lay ahead, but one step they could handle. And then one more, and one more until breathing and living seemed possible again.

I love the quote on their wall: "Life isn't measured by the number of breaths you take, but by the moments that take your breath away." At times, don't you find yourself just breathing and not really living? Maybe life has just gotten very busy with jobs, kids, errands, activities, and routines and you've found yourself sleepwalking through it all. You create a safe zone where you can manage the ups and downs in a carefully controlled range that's comfortable and reduces risk. Sound familiar? I'd argue that's not really living life to its fullest, but it's your life to live and your choice. How do you want to live it? I want to be able count as many moments that take my breath away as possible. Perhaps this quote from Hunter S. Thompson in *Hells Angels* says it best: "Life should not be a journey to the grave with the intention of arriving safely in a pretty and well preserved body, but rather to skid in broadside in a cloud of smoke, thoroughly used up, totally worn out, and loudly proclaiming 'Wow! What a Ride!'"

GETTING NAKED

1. What events in your life have taken your breath away? Which ones were joyful and happy? Which ones were painful and difficult?

2. Do you tend to cope by withdrawing into a shell or by taking one step at a time? Do you react differently depending on whether the "breathtaking" situation is positive or negative? If so, how?

3. Do you relate to having friends named "Anxiety" and "Worry"? How do you handle them?

4. What can you do differently over the next two weeks to change your approach to life from sleepwalking to really living?

5. What would your life look like if you followed the advice quoted above? Remember that each person's "ride" may look and feel different, and that's okay!

Epilogue

Final Thoughts on Getting Real

"Get real!" This exclamation could be a mantra for our lives today and the world we live in. We'd certainly like to tell some of our politicians to "get real." The same goes for those companies and CEOs who indulged in risky investments and business dealings that put our entire economy at risk. And how about reality TV shows—many of them could use a strong dose of "get real" too.

But the starting point for getting real is you and me. Real is different for everyone, because we each have unique personalities and life experiences. Real is shaped by things such as how we grew up, the values passed on from family and faith, the friends we make, our choice of a spouse or partner, our experiences raising a family, love won or lost, career successes and frustrations, our health and that of those close to us, and much more. Learning to "get real" means finding and being your true self—including imperfections—rather than trying to be someone you think you're supposed to be.

One of my favorite stories has always been *The Velveteen Rabbit* by Margery Williams. Through her main characters—two stuffed animals in a child's nursery—Williams explains that becoming real is a process that takes time. It involves getting roughed up a bit, experiencing pain, loving and being loved.

"What is REAL?" asked the Rabbit one day, when they were lying side by side near the nursery fender, before Nana came to tidy the room. "Does it mean having things that buzz inside you and a stick-out handle?"

"Real isn't how you are made," said the Skin Horse. "It's a thing that happens to you. When a child loves you for a long, long time, not just to play with, but REALLY loves you, then you become Real."

"Does it hurt?" asked the Rabbit.

"Sometimes," said the Skin Horse, for he was always truthful. "When you are Real you don't mind being hurt."

"Does it happen all at once, like being wound up," he asked, "or bit by bit?"

"It doesn't happen all at once," said the Skin Horse. "You become. It takes a long time. That's why it doesn't happen often to people who break easily, or have sharp edges, or who have to be carefully kept. Generally, by the time you are Real, most of your hair has been loved off, and your eyes drop out and you get loose in the joints and very shabby. But these things don't matter at all, because once you are Real you can't be ugly, except to people who don't understand."

When we started the journey at the beginning of this book, we asked you to picture your perfect day—what it felt like, looked like, who was with you, what you were thinking, and so on. Maybe you imagined walking on the beach, or feeling the soft blades of grass on the soles of your feet, or simply kicking your shoes off at the end of a satisfying day. Times like these are when you're in the naked-feet state of being—when you are most real. We challenged you to discover more about your real self and to bring that self into your life, both in your workplace and outside of work.

Let me share the stories of two people I have worked with—one who has yet to discover how to be real, and another who is one of the most real people I know. Paul spent a lot of time trying to act the part of being on the fast track at work. He was quick to share stories of his fraternity involvement in college, went out of his way to use (and often misuse) bigger words than necessary, and practiced an exaggerated politeness that came across as fake and condescending. My grandparents would have called this "putting on airs." Unfortunately, Paul was totally unaware that his employees didn't respect him and his fellow supervisors didn't trust him. He actually had the potential to be highly successful, but he was so busy trying to play the part he thought was expected of him that the people around him didn't know who he really was and wouldn't follow him.

Contrast this with Mark—a heavily tattooed military veteran and former disc jockey for a rock radio station. Although he's an immensely talented web designer and graphic artist, when I met Mark he was working in an entry-level administrative job while taking college classes part-time. He had no outward signs of power—no important title, no high-status position—but he was one of the most self-assured people I had ever met. He was unfailingly positive around his coworkers, always offering to help them with their home computers or other electronics issues. He asked them about their families and outside activities and was genuinely interested in what they had to say. He was comfortable being real with those around him, and he knew that where he was at that time didn't define where he was going.

Mark interviewed for several jobs in his field more suited to his talents, but just missed getting hired each time. He took each setback in stride, saying "At least a few more people got to know me and what I have to offer." Recently Mark got a significant promotion to a job that uses his creative skills, and on the side he's working as a freelance web designer and graphic artist. The best part is that he hasn't changed one bit. He still has a quiet self-assurance and genuineness that draws others to him.

The lesson in all of this is that becoming real isn't a quick or easy process. The journey can be difficult, full of ups and downs and detours. Sometimes you get bruised, and maybe a little fur gets rubbed off. But you are not on this earth simply to do a job, make money, acquire things, and play a role that others expect of you. You are here to discover your real self—who you are at your core, what excites you, inspires you, brings you happiness—and to learn from all the experiences that make up your life. You are here to be yourself and to share your real self with others, creating an environment that will nourish, inspire, and challenge yourself and others to be more real—more in line with your naked feet state of mind. May you make the time to enjoy your journey!

End Notes

1   Ziglar, Zig. *See You at the Top*. Gretna, LA: Pelican Publishing Company, Inc, 2005.

2   Delgado, Debbie. Quote from online newsletter "IdealLife Lessons", Volume 1, Issue 20, November 6, 2009. Found at www.DebbieDelgado.com.

3   Thompson, Hunter S. *Hells Angels: A Strange and Terrible Saga*. New York, NY: Ballantine Books, 1995.

4   Williams, Margery. *The Velveteen Rabbit*. New York, NY: Bantam Doubleday Dell Publishing Group, Inc, 1922.

47450431R00057

Made in the USA
Middletown, DE
25 August 2017